50 GREATEST HYMNS

- A Mighty Fortress Is Our God
- Abide with Me
- All Creatures of Our God and King
- All Hail the Power of Jesus' Name
- Alleluia! Alleluia! (Ode to Joy)
- Amazing Grace
- Are You Washed in the Blood?
- At the Cross
- Be Thou My Vision
- Blessed Assurance
- Christ Arose (Low in the Grave He Lay)
- Christ the Lord is Risen Today
- Come, Christians, Join to Sing
- Come, Thou Fount of Every Blessing
- Come, Thou Long-Expected Jesus
- Crown Him with Many Crowns
- Down at the Cross
- Fairest Lord Jesus
- He Leadeth Me
- He Lives (I Know That My Redeemer Lives!)
- Holy, Holy, Holy
- How Great Thou Art
- I Stand Amazed in the Presence (How Marvelous)
- In the Garden
- It Is Well with My Soul

- Jesus Loves Me
- Jesus Paid It All
- Jesus Saves
- Just as I Am
- Love Divine, All Loves Excelling
- My Hope Is Built On Nothing Less
- Near the Cross
- Nearer, My God, to Thee
- Nothing but the Blood
- O For A Thousand Tongues To Sing
- O Sacred Head, Now Wounded
- O the Blood of Jesus
- O Worship the King
- Onward, Christian Soldiers
- Rock Of Ages
- Shall We Gather at the River
- Tell Me the Story of Jesus
- The Old Rugged Cross
- There is a Fountain
- To God Be the Glory
- We Gather Together
- Were You There
- What A Friend We Have in Jesus
- What Wondrous Love Is This
- When I Survey the Wondrous Cross

Arranged by B. C. Dockery

A Mighty Fortress Is Our God

Martin Luther

B. C. Dockery

Arr. ©2022

Abide with Me

William H. Monk
arr. B. C. Dockery

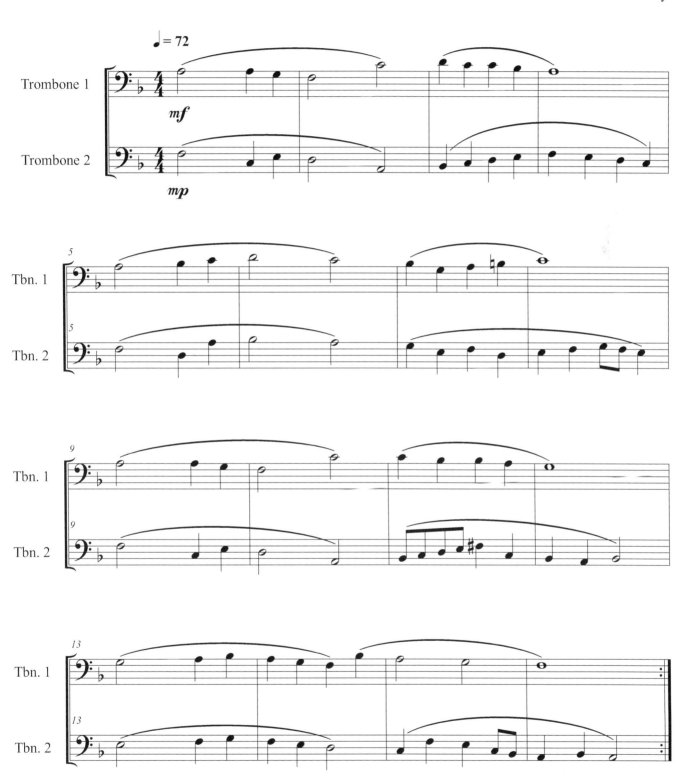

All Creatures of Our God and King

Geistliche Kirchengesang, 1623
arr. B . C. Dockery

All Hail the Power of Jesus' Name

Oliver Holden

B. C. Dockery

Ode to Joy
(Joyful, Joyful, We Adore Thee)

Beethoven
arr. B. C. Dockery

Amazing Grace

John Newton
B. C. Dockery

Are You Washed in the Blood?

Elisha A. Hoffman
arr. B. C. Dockery

At the Cross

Anon
arr. B. C. Dockery

Be Thou My Vision

Traditional
B. C. Dockery

Blessed Assurance

Phoebe P. Knapp
B. C. Dockery

Christ Arose
(Low in the Grave He Lay)

Robert Lowry
arr. B. C. Dockery

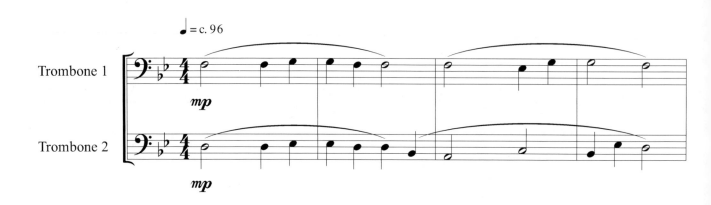

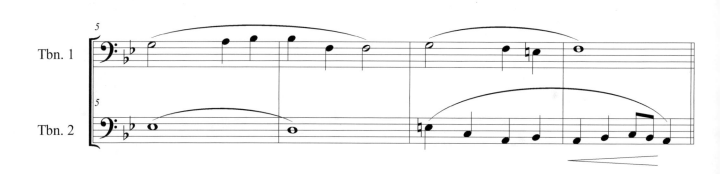

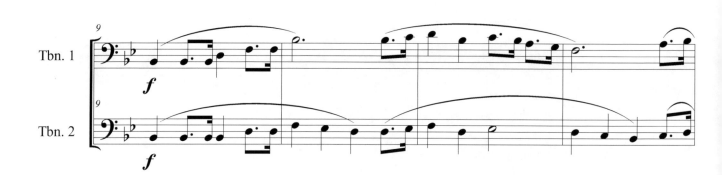

Christ Arose
(Low in the Grave He Lay)

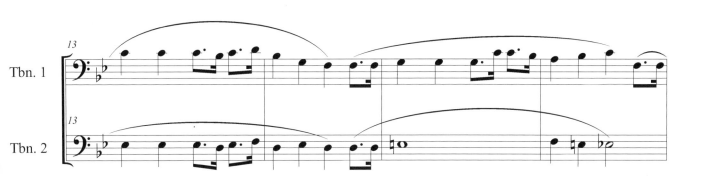

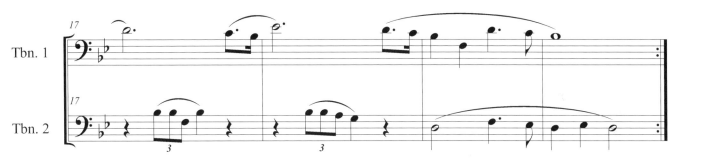

Christ the Lord is Risen Today

Charles Wesley
arr. B. C. Dockery

Come, Christians, Join to Sing

Traditional Spanish Melody
arr. B. C. Dockery

Come, Thou Fount of Every Blessing

Traditional

B. C. Dockery

Come, Thou Long-Expected Jesus

Rowland H. Prichard

B. C. Dockery

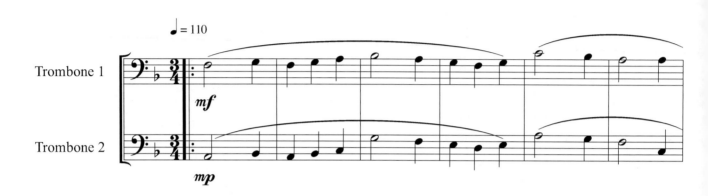

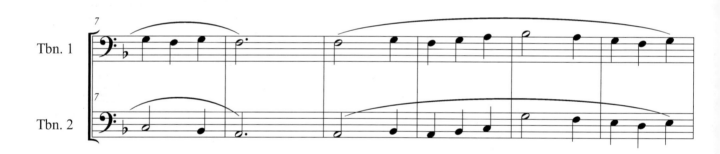

Come, Thou Long-Expected Jesus

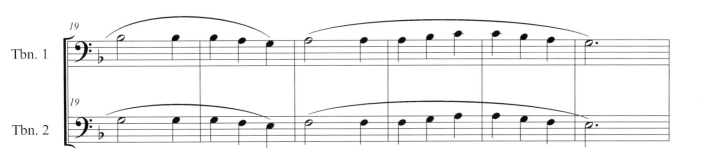

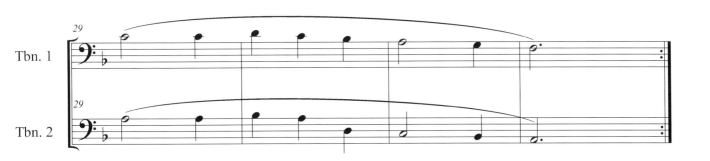

Crown Him with Many Crowns

George J. Elvey

Down at the Cross

John H. Stockton
arr. B. C. Dockery

Fairest Lord Jesus

Silesian Folk Melody
arr. B. C. Dockery

He Leadeth Me

William B. Bradbury

B. C. Dockery

He Lives
(I Know That My Redeemer Lives!)

Samuel Medley
arr. B. C. Dockery

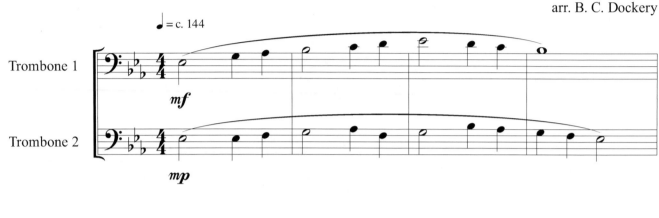

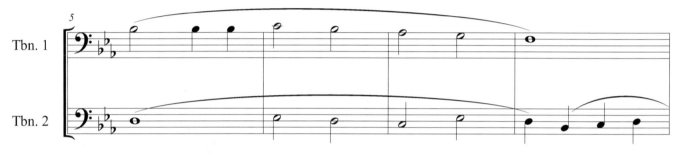

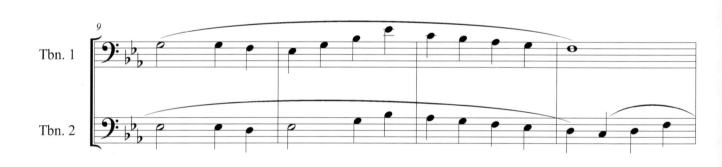

Holy, Holy, Holy

John B. Dykes

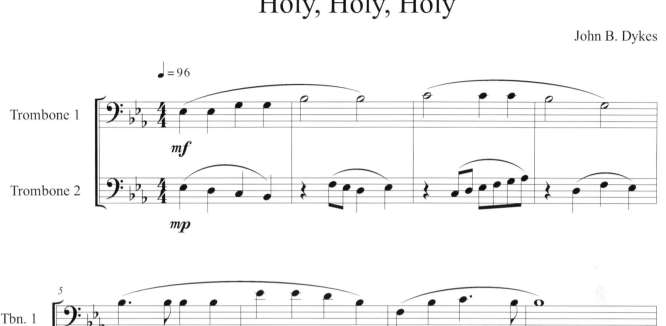

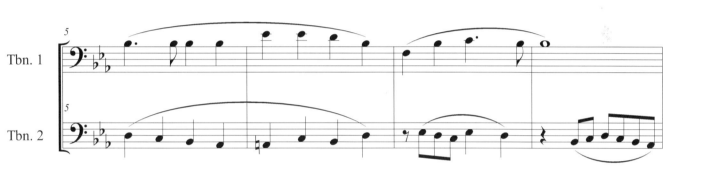

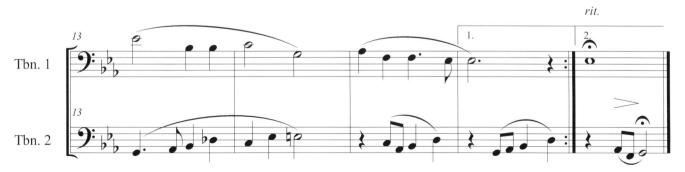

How Great Thou Art

Traditional
B. C. Dockery

I Stand Amazed in the Presence (How Marvelous)

Charles H. Gabriel
arr. B. C. Dockery

In the Garden

C. Austin Miles
arr. B. C. Dockery

It Is Well with My Soul

Philip P. Bliss
B. C. Dockery

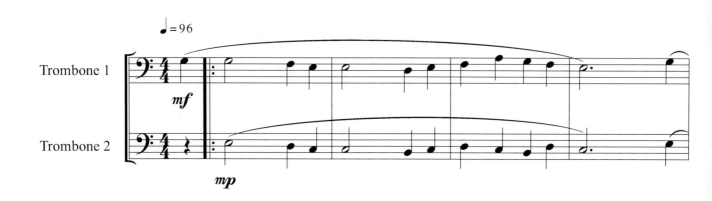

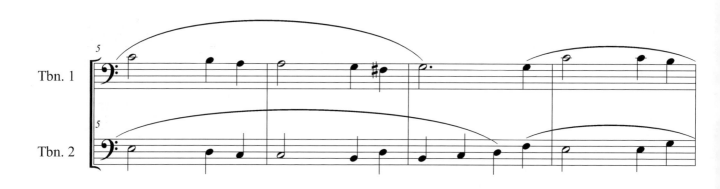

Arr. ©2023

It Is Well with My Soul

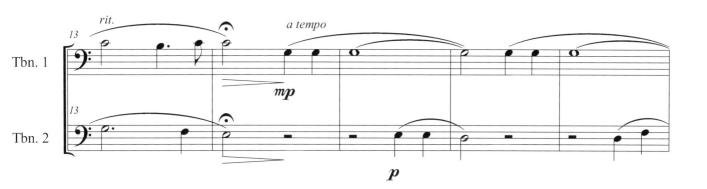

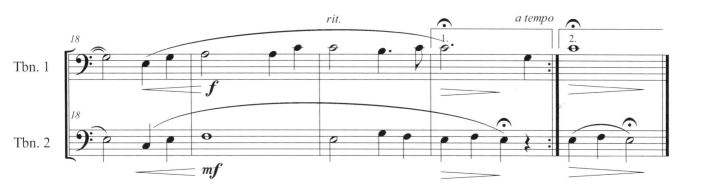

Jesus Loves Me

William B. Bradbury

Jesus Paid It All

John T. Grape
arr. B. C. Dockery

Jesus Saves

We Have Heard the Joyful Sound

William J. Kirkpatrick
arr. B. C. Dockery

Just as I Am

William B. Bradbury

B. C. Dockery

Arr. ©2023

Love Divine, All Loves Excelling

John Zundel

B. C. Dockery

My Hope Is Built On Nothing Less

William B. Bradbury

B. C. Dockery

Arr. ©2023

Near the Cross

William H. Doane
arr. B. C. Dockery

Nearer, My God, to Thee

Lowell Mason

B. C. Dockery

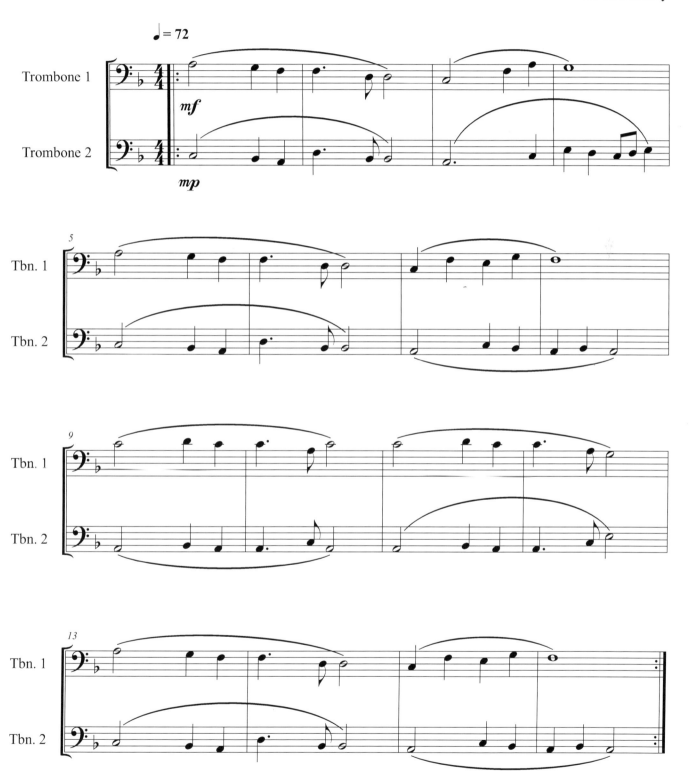

Nothing but the Blood

Robert Lowry
arr. B. C. Dockery

O for a Thousand Tongues to Sing

Carl G. Glazer
B. C. Dockery

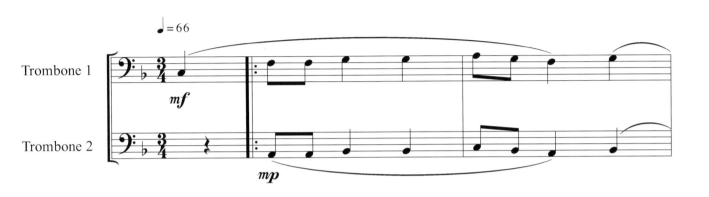

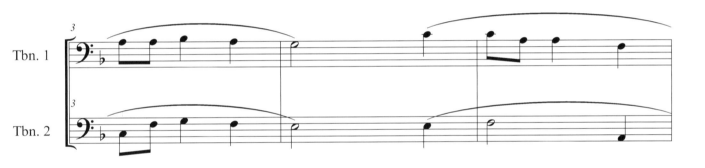

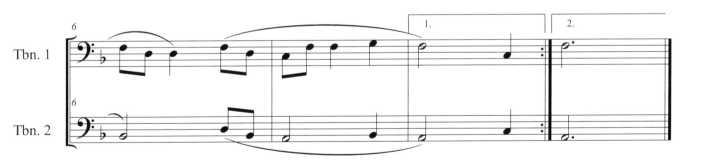

Arr. ©2023

O Sacred Head, Now Wounded

Hans L. Hassler, harmonized by J. S. Bach

arr. B. C. Dockery

O the Blood

Traditional
arr. B. C. Dockery

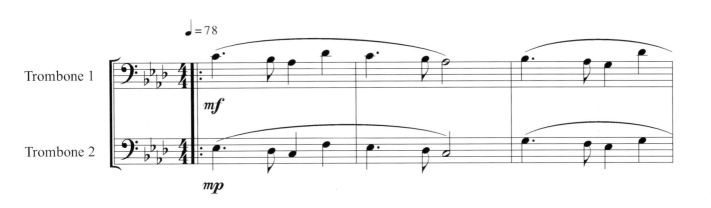

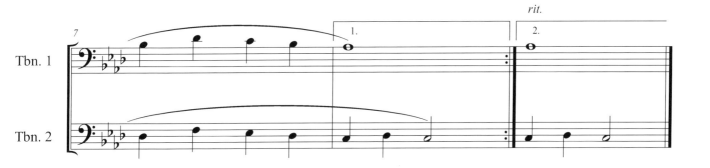

O Worship the King

Attr. Kraus & Haydn
B. C. Dockery

Onward, Christian Soldiers

Arthur S. Sullivan
B. C. Dockery

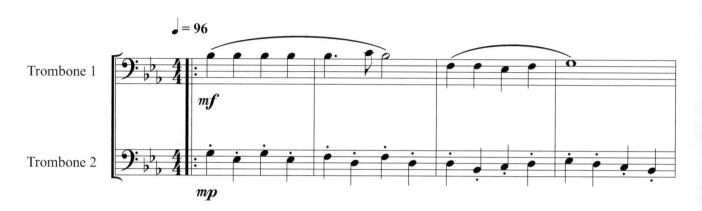

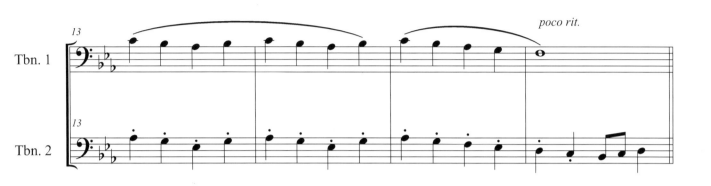

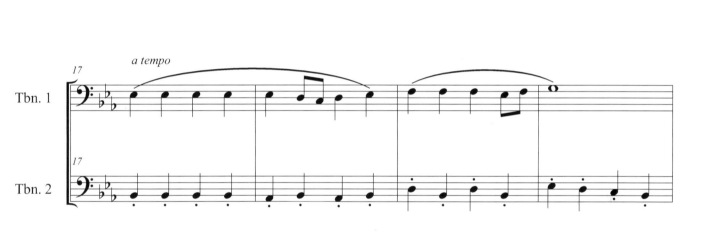

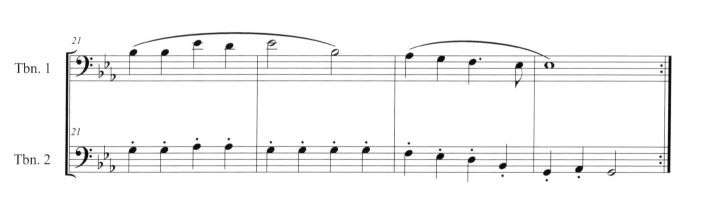

Rock of Ages

Thomas Hastings
B. C. Dockery

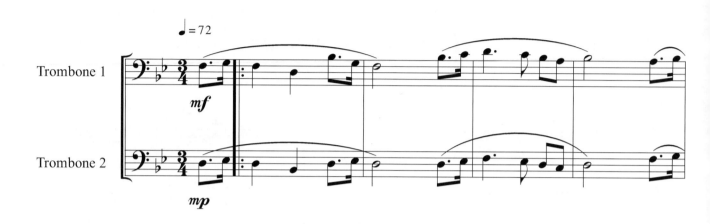

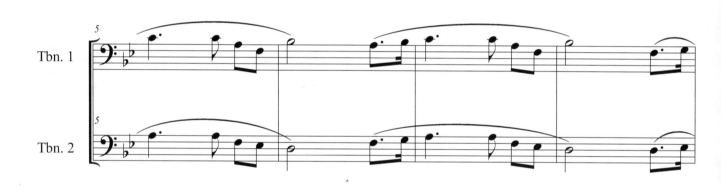

Arr. ©2023

Shall We Gather at the River

Robert Lowry
Arr. B. C. Dockery

Tell Me the Story of Jesus

John R. Sweney

arr. B. C. Dockery

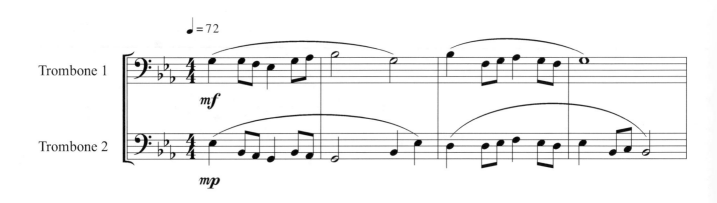

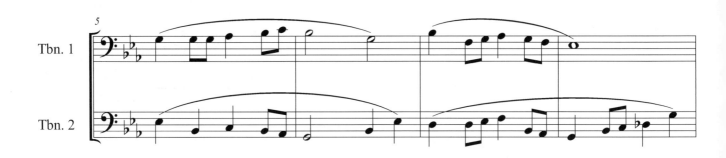

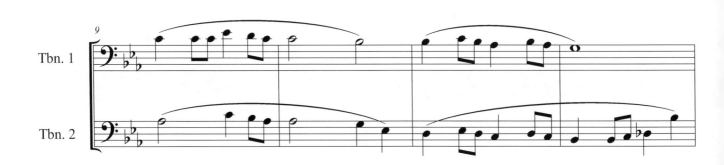

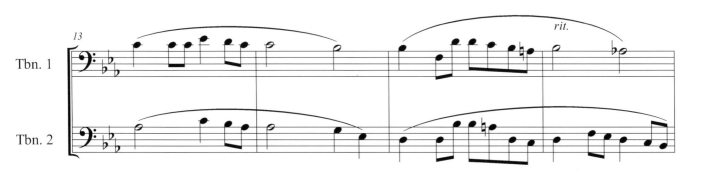

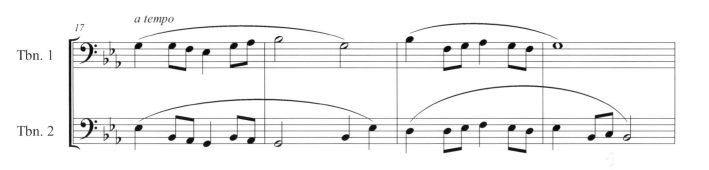

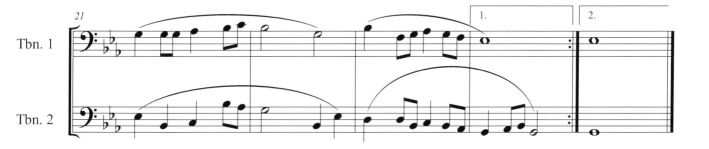

The Old Rugged Cross

George Bennard
arr. B. C. Dockery

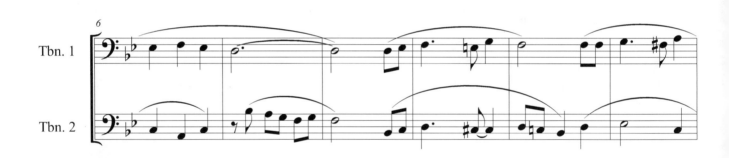

The Old Rugged Cross

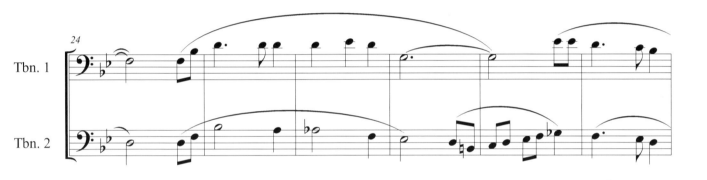

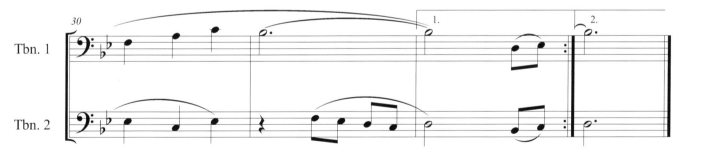

There Is a Fountain

Traditional
arr. B. C. Dockery

To God Be the Glory

William H. Doane

B. C. Dockery

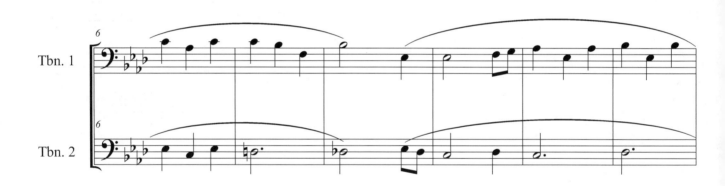

Arr. ©2023

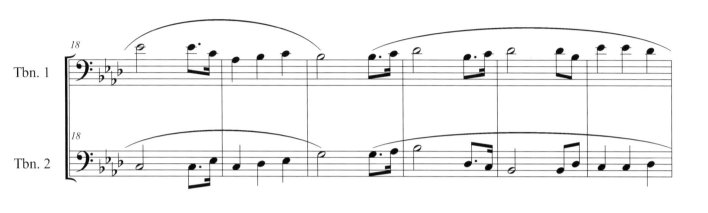

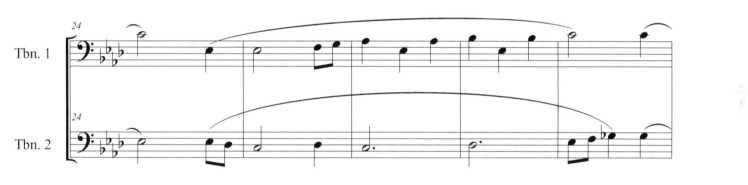

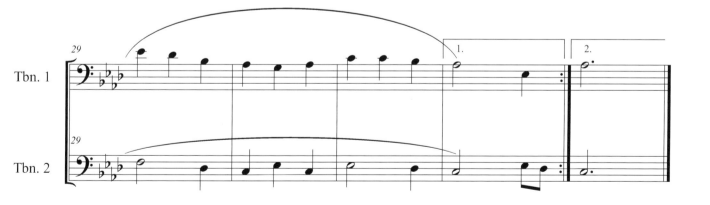

We Gather Together

Dutch Folk Tune
Arr. by B. C. Dockery

Were You There

Traditional
arr. B. C. Dockery

What a Friend We Have in Jesus

Charles C. Converse

B. C. Dockery

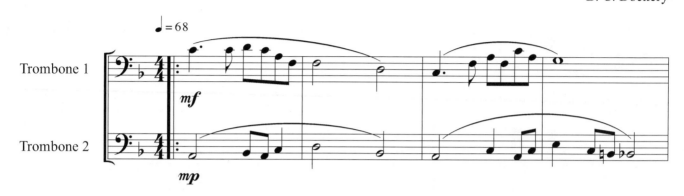

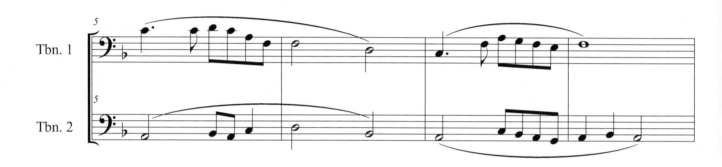

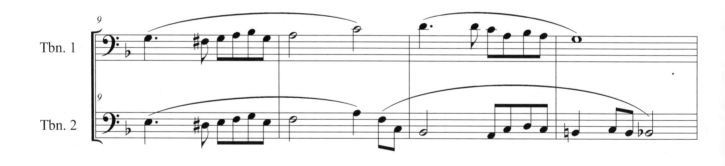

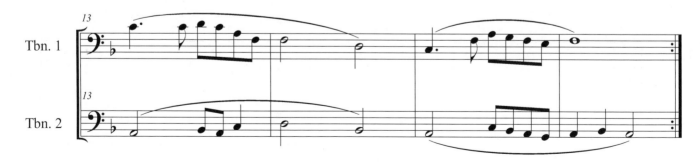

What Wondrous Love Is This

Anonymous

Arr. by B. C. Dockery

When I Survey the Wondrous Cross

Lowell Mason
arr. B. C. Dockery

Made in United States
Orlando, FL
18 December 2024

56000062R00037